SHANNON LUCID

SHANNON LUCID

SPACE AMBASSADOR

CARMEN BREDESON

A Gateway Biography
The Millbrook Press
Brookfield, Connecticut

Cover photographs courtesy of NASA and AP/Wide World.

Photographs courtesy of NASA: pp. 8, 15, 21, 25,
27, 28, 29, 33, 34, 35; Sygma: pp. 10 (© L. Downing), 17, 38, 40
(© F. Carter-Smith); Bethany High School: p. 12;
Sovfoto/Eastfoto: p. 13.

Library of Congress Cataloging-in-Publication Data
Bredeson, Carmen.
Shannon Lucid : space ambassador / Carmen Bredeson.
p. cm. — (A Gateway biography)
Includes bibliographical references and index.
Summary: Chronicles the life of the astronaut from her childhood
in Oklahoma through her various space shuttle missions to her
six months aboard the Mir space station.
ISBN 0-7613-0406-1 (lib. bdg.)
1. Lucid, Shannon, 1943– —Juvenile literature.
2. Women astronauts—United States—Biography—Juvenile
literature. [1. Lucid, Shannon, 1943– . 2. Astronauts.
3. Women—Biography.]
I. Title. II. Series.
TL789.85.L83B74 1998
629.45'0092—dc21   [B] 97-47147 CIP AC

Published by The Millbrook Press, Inc.
2 Old New Milford Road
Brookfield, Connecticut 06804

SHANNON LUCID

A medical rescue team stood near the runway, waiting for the arrival of the space shuttle *Atlantis*. Two of the medics practiced locking their arms together to make a seat. They planned to carry Shannon Lucid off the shuttle. The fifty-three-year-old astronaut had been orbiting the Earth aboard the Russian space station *Mir* for more than six months. After being weightless for so long, nobody expected her to be able to walk.

As the medics watched, *Atlantis* glided into view and made a perfect landing at the Kennedy Space Center in Florida. Inside the shuttle, Lucid remained strapped into her seat. With Earth's gravity once again pulling her body down, her arms and legs felt very heavy and she was a little dizzy.

The space shuttle Atlantis touches down at
Kennedy Space Center in Florida on September 26, 1996.
Among the astronauts inside is Shannon Lucid,
returning from her nearly six-month mission aboard
the Russian space station Mir.

When the medics entered *Atlantis,* they found that Shannon Lucid was indeed having some difficulty. Her problem was not caused by gravity, though. The helmet to her space suit was stuck on her head. Two NASA technicians were trying to pry it loose with a pair of pliers and a screwdriver. It took them fifteen minutes to get the helmet off. Finally, the medics could carry Lucid out of the shuttle. When they approached her she amazed them by saying, "No, I can stand up." With a little support from the two men, Shannon Lucid stood and walked out of *Atlantis* to the crew transporter!

Lucid's husband, Mike, and their children—Kawai, age twenty-eight, Shani, age twenty-six, and Michael, age twenty-one—were eagerly waiting to greet the returning astronaut. When Mike was asked about the amazing feat his wife had performed in walking out of *Atlantis*, he said, "She wouldn't let something like gravity stop her. She always pushes herself to the limit."

The day after *Atlantis* landed, the Lucid family boarded an airplane bound for Ellington Field, located near Houston, Texas. Among the large crowd waiting for their arrival were many of Lucid's co-workers, along with President Bill Clinton. He was there to welcome the United States' most experienced astronaut back to Earth. Her 188-day *Mir* mission, along with four other flights, gave Lucid 223 total days in space, more than any other American astronaut.

In his remarks to the crowd about Dr. Shannon Lucid, Clinton said: "Perhaps more than even she knows, she set a remarkable example for a new generation of young Americans, espe-

President Bill Clinton welcomed Shannon Lucid
and the other Mir astronauts home. He praised Lucid as a
remarkable example for a new generation of young Americans,
and gave her a huge box of M&Ms, her favorite candy,
as a welcome-home gift.

cially young women, who look up to her and see possibilities that are new and uncharted for their own lives. Our young people, like those who are here today, will be doing work that hasn't been invented yet."

When Shannon Lucid was a child, space travel had not yet been invented, except in the minds of science-fiction writers.

EYES ON THE SKY

Shannon Wells was born in China on January 14, 1943. Her father was a Baptist preacher in Shanghai, and her mother was a missionary nurse.

At the time of Shannon's birth, World War II was in progress. Parts of China, including Shanghai, had been invaded and occupied by the Japanese. Since Japan was also at war with the United States, many Americans living in China were rounded up and put into camps.

The Wells family spent a year in one of the camps before being exchanged for some Japanese prisoners who were being held by the United States. After their release, the Wells family returned to America. At the war's end in 1945 they went back to China, but had to leave again when Communists took control of the country in 1949.

Mr. and Mrs. Wells moved to Bethany, Oklahoma, with their daughter. During her childhood in Bethany, Shannon enjoyed reading about the people who explored the American frontier. She said: "I always wanted to be an explorer, a pioneer. I wanted to discover a lost continent, but there weren't any lost continents." Shannon thought that she had been born at the wrong time until she read a book about Robert Goddard, the famous rocket scientist. When she finished the book, she thought: "Well, shoot, I can be a space explorer. Nobody's going to get space all explored before I grow up." Shannon told one of her teachers that she wanted to travel in space. The teacher replied that the job didn't exist, and even if it did, a girl wouldn't be able to do it.

Shannon Wells did not give up her dream, though. She sold her bicycle to buy a telescope so that she could get a better look at the sky. On starry nights in Oklahoma, Shannon spent hours studying the lights that looked down on her from space. When she was fourteen years old, a new object took its place in space, an object put there by human beings.

On October 4, 1957, the Soviet Union blasted an artificial

As a young girl, Shannon Lucid wanted to be an explorer. Space travel was brand new when she graduated from Bethany High School in 1960, but that did not keep her from dreaming of doing it herself.

satellite into orbit around Earth. The launch of *Sputnik I* stunned the world. Even though it was only 23 inches (58 centimeters) in diameter, *Sputnik I* was the first man-made object sent into orbit. Every 96 minutes, the 195-pound (88-kilogram) satellite made

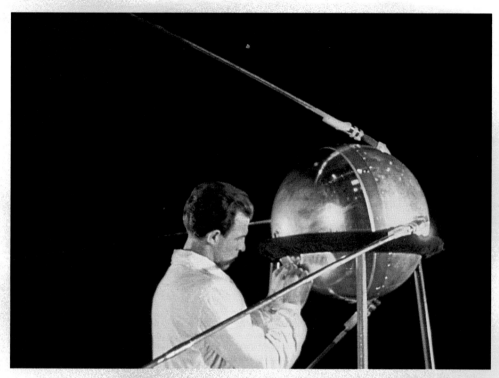

Sputnik I, *a satellite launched by the Soviet Union in 1957, was the first man-made object to orbit Earth. Although it doesn't look too important by today's standards, its launch signaled the beginning of the space race between the United States and its former rival.*

one complete circle of Earth. American scientists were determined to catch up with the Russians. They put their programs into high gear, and the space race was on.

The United States created the National Aeronautics and Space Administration (NASA). NASA immediately started looking for test pilots who were qualified to become astronauts. Hundreds of men applied to the program and went through rigorous testing. On April 9, 1959, seven men were chosen to be America's first astronauts. Shannon Wells wrote a letter to *Time* magazine asking why no women were eligible for the astronaut program. She later said: "I couldn't believe it when they selected the first seven [*Mercury* astronauts]. I mean, it was incredible, the feeling of anger, because there were no females included in the selection."

With her eyes still on the sky, Shannon began taking flying lessons after graduating from high school in 1960. While attending the University of Oklahoma, she had a number of part-time jobs to pay for the ten-dollar-an-hour lessons. She kept at it though, and finally got her pilot's license. Shannon bought an old Piper Clipper airplane and sometimes flew her father to church revivals in nearby towns.

While at college, Shannon majored in chemistry. She decided on that subject, she said, "because when I was in the fourth grade someone told me that water was composed of hydrogen and oxygen, and I thought it was absolutely amazing that two gases would form a liquid." After her graduation in 1963, Shannon worked as a laboratory technician for a medical research company.

Three years later Shannon Wells changed jobs and went to work for Kerr-McGee, an oil company in Oklahoma City. It was there that she met Mike Lucid, who was a research chemist at the company. Shannon said that Mike "…called me up one

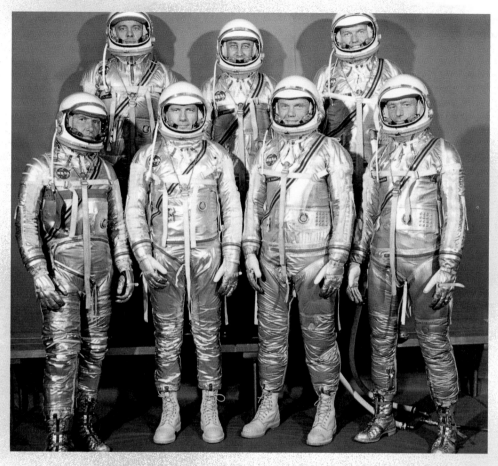

The first seven astronauts selected by the National Aeronautics and Space Administration (NASA) in 1959 for the Mercury program were (first row, left to right) Walter Schirra, Donald Slayton, John Glenn, M. Scott Carpenter, and (back row) Alan Shepard, Virgil Grissom, and L. Gordon Cooper. Shannon Lucid, fourteen years old at the time, was discouraged that no women were eligible for the mission.

Sunday and wanted to go out. I had been planning on flying, but the weather was too bad so I couldn't go. Instead, we went to a boat show. Nine months later, we were married."

Shannon Lucid left Kerr-McGee after the couple's first child, Kawai Dawn, was born on September 19, 1968. Shortly after her daughter's birth, Lucid began attending classes again at the University of Oklahoma. She earned a master's degree in biochemistry in 1970. The same year, a second daughter, Shandara Michelle, was born (on January 13). She went on to get her Ph.D. in biochemistry in 1973. A third child, Michael Kermit, was born to the Lucids on August 22, 1975. With her education and family complete, Lucid went to work in the area of health science and medical research. Then, in 1978, NASA made a decision that would change the direction of Shannon Lucid's life.

ASTRONAUT TRAINING

After nearly twenty years of accepting only men into the astronaut program, NASA opened the doors to women applicants. In the past, astronaut candidates had to have test-flight experience. There were no women test pilots at the time, so women were not eligible for the program. In 1978, NASA decided to have two types of astronauts. Pilots would still fly and command the spacecraft, but mission specialists would also be part of the crew. With backgrounds in science, medicine, and engineering,

In 1978, NASA changed their requirements for astronauts and women were now given the chance to go through the training. Shannon Lucid was one of six women to do so that year. Pictured here are (left to right): Rhea Seddon, Anna Fisher, Judith Resnik, Lucid, Sally Ride, and Kathryn Sullivan, the first women astronauts.

they would perform experiments in the weightlessness of space as part of their duties.

Shannon Lucid's education in biochemistry qualified her for the astronaut program. She quickly filled out an application and sent it to NASA. A few months later, Lucid was notified that she was one of the first six women to be accepted into the astronaut training program. Shannon was the only woman in the program who had children. A reporter asked her if being an astronaut wasn't too dangerous a job for a mother. She replied that most of the astronauts in the program had children. "They were dads."

Since astronaut training took place at the Johnson Space Center in Houston, the Lucids packed up their belongings and moved from Oklahoma to Texas. During the next year the six women, along with the other astronaut candidates, went through rigorous testing to see whether they had what it took to fly in space. Their hearing, vision, and overall fitness were measured. They were whirled around in a giant centrifuge to simulate the pressure that astronauts feel during liftoff and reentry.

The trainees were also taken up in the cargo hold of a KC-135 transport plane. The plane leveled off at 25,000 feet (40,230 kilometers) and then started to climb at a sharp angle. It flew up to 32,000 feet (51,500 kilometers) and then started to dive back down to 25,000 feet again. During much of the rapid ascent and descent, the passengers inside the cabin were weight-less. This up-and-down maneuver was done over and over, some-times more than 40 times. During their first experiences with weightlessness, many astronaut trainees feel nauseated, which is why the plane is often called the "Vomit Comet."

Shannon Lucid passed all the tests with flying colors and was officially named an astronaut in August 1979. At the time Lucid joined NASA, the $10 billion space shuttle program was just getting under way. The shuttle was designed to be the first reusable spacecraft. It would be launched with a rocket like other spacecraft, but would be able to return to Earth and land when the mission was finished. While in orbit it could be used as a laboratory for scientific experiments. The shuttle astronauts on board could also launch commercial satellites into orbit and repair satellites that had been damaged.

The first shuttle flight of *Columbia* would not take place until 1981. Until that time, Shannon Lucid performed several jobs connected with the shuttle program. For a while she helped test the computer software that controlled the missions. Among her other assignments, Lucid worked as a spacecraft communicator in Mission Control and helped test different parts of the space shuttle. In all, she would train and prepare for seven long years before finally flying in space. Her first mission would be on *Discovery*, which was scheduled to blast off in the summer of 1985.

LIFTOFF

After all the years of training, the launch date of *Discovery* mission STS-51G finally arrived. A week before scheduled liftoff, Shannon Lucid and the rest of the crew went into seclusion at the Johnson Space Center. This was done to keep the astronauts from catching colds or other illnesses. Three days before the flight, the crew flew to Cape Canaveral, Florida, the site of the launch. Already in Florida were Mike Lucid and the couple's three children, who were then sixteen, fifteen, and nine years old. They planned to watch the launch and then go to Disney World.

The shuttle crew got up at 3 A.M. on the morning of the flight. After breakfast they began suiting up, which took about an hour. They then got on a bus for a ride to the launchpad. Technicians made a final check of the suits, and the astronauts climbed into the shuttle and were strapped into their seats.

Soon after the final countdown began, massive rockets under *Discovery* began to belch fire and smoke into the air. Shannon Lucid's family was 3 miles (5 kilometers) away, watching the liftoff from the top of the Launch Control Center. Mike Lucid said: "At T-minus four things got pretty intense. Our eyes were riveted to the launchpad. The rockets ignited and the *Discovery* leaped a mile into the air in seconds. The enormous roar of the rockets hit us and shook the building. We were spellbound."

Nine minutes after liftoff, the main engines cut off as *Discovery* slipped into orbit 220 miles (354 kilometers) above the Earth. Once safely in orbit the crew unfastened the straps that held them securely in their seats. They changed into their flight suits, which consisted of a navy blue T-shirt, a pair of light blue cotton pants, and a zippered jacket. Once dressed, it was time to go to work.

The shuttle is divided into three levels. On the upper level is the flight deck and several work stations. Living quarters are located on the mid-deck. Here the crew eats, sleeps, and performs experiments. The lower deck contains the equipment necessary for the flight, such as the air purification system.

Shannon Lucid's first mission came in 1985 aboard the space shuttle Discovery, *where she worked as a mission specialist. One of her duties was to measure the effects of weightlessness on the shuttle's crew. Floating through the ship's mid-deck area, Lucid watches as other astronauts adjust some equipment.*

Each crew member wears a headset to communicate with the other astronauts and with mission control.

Shannon Lucid was a mission specialist on the *Discovery* flight. One of her jobs was to deploy X-ray equipment to take photographs of the center of the Milky Way. Lucid used the robot arm (50 feet, or 15 meters, long), located in the shuttle's cargo bay, to deposit the equipment in space. She also helped measure the effect of weightlessness on the hearts of the shuttle crew.

In addition to their other jobs, the astronauts also had to do a lot of housekeeping chores. Everyday activities, such as preparing food, take longer in space. Most of the food used on the shuttle has been dehydrated to remove the liquid, because dried food takes up less space. Each package of dried food has to have the water mixed back in before it is eaten. Warm water is injected into the package through a hollow needle. The package is kneaded to mix the contents and then heated in an oven.

Drinks on the shuttle are in powdered form. Water is added to the package, and the drink is sipped through a straw to keep the liquid from floating away. Shannon Lucid and the other astronauts select their own menus before each shuttle mission from more than one hundred food choices and twenty different drink selections.

Washing in space is also time-consuming. On Earth, the force of gravity pulls water down so that it runs off the body. In space, water either spreads out on the skin or floats. Instead of showering, the shuttle astronauts take sponge baths to keep clean. They have to use a cloth to spread water on their skin, then apply soap and rub, then wipe the soap away, and spread more water to rinse.

To use the bathroom, crew members urinate into a funnel-shaped device that acts like a vacuum and pulls the liquid into a collection bag. To defecate, there is a toilet seat to sit on. The solid matter is sucked into a container that is disposed of after the flight is over. If there is a problem with the system, individual bags are available for each astronaut to use.

When it is time to go to sleep, each crew member has a personal sleeping bag. Since there is no up or down in weightlessness, the bag can be attached to the ceiling, wall, or floor. The bag is zipped up to the neck, and straps are fastened across the forehead to keep the astronaut's head from bobbing around. Some astronauts use eye masks and ear plugs to keep out the light and noise.

With all the work to do aboard the space shuttle, the missions usually go by very quickly. Even though *Discovery* made 112 orbits of Earth, it was soon time for Shannon Lucid and the crew to head home. The astronauts put on their reentry suits and strapped themselves into their seats about 45 minutes before touchdown. The orbital maneuvering system engines were fired to slow *Discovery* from its speed of 17,500 miles (28,160 kilometers) per hour. As the shuttle slowed down, it dropped lower and lower until it entered the atmosphere around Earth. *Discovery* glided onto the runway at Edwards Air Force Base in California on June 24, 1985.

Just seven months after Lucid's first mission, disaster struck the space program. Seventy-three seconds after liftoff, the space shuttle *Challenger* exploded, killing the crew, which included the first teacher in space, Christa McAuliffe. Another astronaut who lost her life was Judith Resnik. She had been one of the first six women astronauts, along with Shannon Lucid, Rhea Seddon, Sally Ride, Kathryn Sullivan, and Anna Fisher.

After the *Challenger* tragedy, all future shuttle flights were canceled while the entire program was closely examined. Many changes were made in shuttle design and operation to provide greater safety for the crews. It was nearly three years before another shuttle mission was attempted. The flight of *Discovery* on September 29, 1988, marked America's return to space.

Shannon Lucid's second flight, STS-34, was aboard the space shuttle *Atlantis*, which lifted off on October 18, 1989. On that mission, the crew deployed the *Galileo* spacecraft, which was sent to explore the planet Jupiter. Lucid also flew on two more shuttle missions, STS-43 in 1991 and STS-58 in 1993. She had logged 558 orbits of Earth in four flights before being selected to join the Russian cosmonauts (as Russian astronauts are called) aboard the space station *Mir*.

LIFE ABOARD *MIR*

The first module of the Russian space station *Mir* was launched on February 20, 1986. Since that time, six other sections have been added to the station's docking ports. A series of cosmo-

Sleeping on the space shuttle is a special challenge that might seem like fun to try. These astronauts, on a Discovery *mission in 1993, are anchored to the walls of the shuttle, although their arms float as they sleep. At the bottom of the picture, one astronaut is almost completely zippered into his "sleep restraint."*

nauts have lived aboard *Mir* continuously since it went into orbit. Flying at a speed of 17,300 miles (27,840 kilometers) per hour, 250 miles (400 kilometers) above Earth, space station *Mir* has served as an orbiting laboratory and observatory for more than a decade.

After the Soviet Union broke up into individual countries in 1991, relations between Russia and the United States started to improve. In an effort to promote cooperation, the space agencies from both countries decided to try an experiment. Russia agreed to let American astronauts live and work on *Mir* in exchange for funds to help keep the aging space station repaired. The first American chosen to join the Russian cosmonauts was astronaut Norman Thagard. His mission on *Mir* lasted a total of 115 days in 1995. The second American astronaut selected to live aboard *Mir* was Shannon Lucid.

In order to prepare for her upcoming flight, Lucid moved to Russia for a year, while her family remained in Houston. She lived at Star City, the cosmonaut training facility, where she studied the Russian language and culture. She also learned about *Mir* and the duties of the cosmonauts. After her year of training was finished, Lucid returned to the United States to continue preparations for her upcoming flight.

On March 22, 1996, Shannon Lucid's adventure began as she lifted off with the crew of the space shuttle *Atlantis*. After docking with the Russian space station, supplies were transferred onto *Mir*, and Lucid entered her new home. She was officially greeted by her Russian hosts, cosmonauts Yuri Onufrienko

Before she could begin her mission aboard Mir, Shannon Lucid went to Russia and lived at Star City, that country's space training facility. In this picture, she emerges from a training spacecraft after learning water survival techniques.

and Yuri Usachev, whom she often affectionately called "the two Yuris."

After being assigned a small space for personal belongings, Shannon quickly settled into life aboard *Mir*. She attached her sleeping bag to one wall and used Velcro to fasten her laptop computer to another. To make the space more like home, she strapped some empty food cartons to the wall to hold her books. She later said that her sleeping area was "…like living in the back of your pickup with your kids…when it's raining and no

Soon after their initial meeting in space aboard Mir, *American astronauts and Russian cosmonauts exchanged gifts of books. Shannon Lucid is among them, third from left.*

Orbiting Earth for more than twelve years, the
Russian space station Mir *has* withstood much damage
and endured the harsh environment of space.
The results of a collision with a supply ship can be seen on
one of the ship's solar array panels in this picture
taken in September 1997.

SPACE FOOD

In the early days of space travel, astronaut food left something to be desired.

Some of it had the consistency of mush and was squeezed directly into the mouth from a tooth-pastelike tube.

Sandwiches were cut into little cubes and coated with clear gelatin so that crumbs would not escape and float around the capsule.

Even though the food was nutritious, it was not very appetizing. Astronaut complaints caused NASA to go back to the drawing board to create better food.

Mealtimes in space gradually improved, and today's shuttle astronauts have a wide variety of food choices.

Today, astronauts on the space shuttle can make their selections from daily menus like those on the facing page:

DAY ONE:

Breakfast	Lunch	Dinner
dried pears	ham	chicken à la king
sausage patty	bread	chicken and rice
scrambled eggs	diced peaches	asparagus
corn flakes	pecan cookies	chocolate
hot cocoa	apple drink	pudding
orange-pineapple drink		grape drink

DAY TWO:

Breakfast	Lunch	Dinner
diced apricots	peanut butter	frankfurters
seasoned scrambled eggs	jelly	potato patty
	bread	green beans
bran flakes	fruit cocktail	broccoli
hot cocoa	fruitcake	strawberries
orange juice mix	tea	vanilla pudding
		tropical punch

All of the shuttle food is in individual packages that fit into slots on a tray. This keeps the astronaut's meal from floating away. Utensils have magnetic strips to keep them on the tray when not in use. The entire tray can be attached to the astronaut's leg with a Velcro strap.

one can get out." Even though *Mir* has several different sections, there is a lot of equipment on board and conditions are crowded.

The crew members ate their meals together in the *Mir* core module. Astronaut Norm Thagard had warned Lucid ahead of time about the Russians' diet of jellied fish and borscht, a kind of soup made from beets. She came prepared with a supply of rice, M&Ms, and Jello. She said "I introduced them to Jello and established it as a Sunday night tradition." She also told them about the Lucid "family tradition of having pizza on Friday night, but unfortunately, we couldn't find anyone who could deliver."

Lucid ended up eating a combination of Russian and American food. One of her favorite Russian dishes was a kind of beef, potato, and vegetable stew that came in cans. Most of the food was canned or dehydrated, so the crew missed fresh fruit and vegetables. Supply ships arrived only about every six weeks to deliver equipment, clothes, and food. After the arrival of one of the ships, the *Mir* crew could smell fresh vegetables as soon as the hatch was opened. Lucid said that they stopped for lunch right then. "We had fresh tomatoes and onions; I never have had such a good lunch. For the next week we had fresh tomatoes three times a day. It was a sad meal when we ate the last ones!"

The crew shared a vacuum-operated toilet and took sponge baths to keep clean. When Shannon Lucid was asked during the mission how she did her laundry and showered, she answered, "Well, you don't. I haven't had a shower since I left,

Shannon Lucid and her Russian crew mates, "the two Yuris," check the food supplies aboard Mir *before* Atlantis, *the shuttle that carried Lucid there, returns to Earth.*

March 22." She also said that "the best thing about doing the laundry is that you don't have to do it. When your clothes get dirty you just throw them away." Mike Lucid jokingly said about his wife that "NASA promised to hose her down before they give her back."

During most of her days on *Mir*, Shannon Lucid performed science experiments. She lit candles and watched to see how fire acted in space, and studied the way quail embryos developed inside their shells. Lucid also planted wheat seeds in a small greenhouse. Many of the experiments were done with spaceflights of many months or years in mind. Astronauts will have to be able to grow food aboard their spacecraft if they ever plan to visit distant planets.

During her time on Mir, *Shannon Lucid performed several science experiments. Some of her experiments had to do with the effects of space on plant and animal development. Here, she checks the progress of some wheat she planted in a small greenhouse.*

Between experiments, Lucid spent a great deal of time exercising on the treadmill and stationary bicycle. Since there is no pressure on the human body in weightlessness, the muscles and bones shrink because they are not being used as much as they were on Earth. Exercise helps prevent some of the loss, so Shannon spent two hours a day working out.

After long days of experiments and exercise, evening was a time for relaxation aboard *Mir*. Shannon Lucid often spent time looking at Earth out of the large window in the *Kvant* module. She stayed in touch with her family at home through NASA

Shannon Lucid works out aboard Mir *on a treadmill device. To keep her bones and muscles strong during her six-month stay in space, she needed to exercise regularly.*

LIFE IN SPACE

When living in a weightless environment like the one aboard a space shuttle or space station like *Mir*, there are many things that are different from life on Earth, such as:

• Astronauts can't stay seated without a strap to hold their body in place.

• Sweat doesn't drip off a person in space. Instead, it pools and collects on various parts of the body. After an exercise period, 1/4 inch (0.64 centimeters) of water may have accumulated on an astronaut's back. It has to be wiped off with a towel.

• When you cut yourself in space, the blood forms a ball over the cut instead of running off. If the cut is a bad one, the blood spreads out on the skin.

• Loose skin on the face tends to rise in space, which can change an astronaut's appearance somewhat. Also, long hair floats and must be tied back to keep it from getting tangled in the equipment.

• Eyeglasses may bob around on the face or even fly off if the head is turned too quickly. Straps help keep them in place.

• The head bobs around during sleep if it is not held down by a strap across the forehead.

video and audio conferences and by exchanging e-mail messages. An avid book lover, Lucid also enjoyed reading in her quarters before going to sleep at night. She said, "Whenever you have a good book, you don't get bored."

Originally, Shannon Lucid was scheduled to stay on *Mir* for 140 days. Her return was delayed once when emergency repairs had to be made to the shuttle's booster rockets. Further delays were caused by two hurricanes that threatened the Florida coast near the Kennedy Space Center. When the delays kept coming, Lucid reacted in her usual calm manner. She simply said, "I'm going to stay up here a little longer, and I'll be home a little bit later."

She did make a request to have some more books and snack foods sent up on the next supply ship. NASA made sure that plenty of M&Ms and Twinkies were sent to Lucid. Her daughters also picked out some new books for their mom to read. Shannon later said that as she was reading one of the books, she "...came to the last page, and the hero, who was being chased by an angry mob, escaped by stepping through a mirror. The end. Continues in Volume Two. And was there Volume Two in my book bag? No. Could I dash out to the bookstore? No. Talk about a feeling of total isolation and frustration."

Before Lucid's ride home arrived, it was time for her Russian crewmates to be replaced by two new cosmonauts. She said good-bye to "the two Yuris" and welcomed Valeriy Korzun and Aleksandr Kaleri to *Mir* on August 19, 1996. They got acquainted and continued working together until *Atlantis* docked with the space station on September 19. After the hatch was

*Shannon looks pleased in this photo taken shortly
before her return to Earth aboard* Atlantis. *After nearly six
months in space, Lucid had turned her Mir duties
over to her replacement, astronaut John Blaha, and
was ready to come home.*

opened, Shannon Lucid greeted the Americans with a tray of bread and salt, the traditional Russian welcome. *Atlantis* spent five days connected to *Mir* while the crews unloaded supplies and equipment.

Finally, after 188 days in space, it was time for Shannon Lucid to return to Earth. Staying behind in her place was American astronaut John Blaha. As *Atlantis* pulled away from *Mir*, Lucid waved good-bye. She later said: "That was my home for six months, and I had a great time there. But, obviously, I was very, very anxious to go back to my real home in Houston, and my family."

WELCOME HOME

After walking on her own out of the space shuttle, Shannon Lucid found a huge box of M&Ms waiting for her in the crew transporter. They were a gift from President Bill Clinton. He later called Lucid to thank her for helping to improve relations between Russia and the United States. He also said: "You've given us all a great deal to be proud of. We're glad you're home safe and sound."

When asked about her most memorable experience aboard *Mir*, Shannon Lucid related a conversation that she had with her two crewmates one day. They were talking about the Cold War and the fact that the Soviet Union and the United States had been enemies for so many years. Lucid said: "It dawned on all

Home at last! Shannon Lucid is accompanied by her family as she arrives in Washington to be honored by President Clinton. Left to right are Mike Lucid, her husband; son-in-law Jeff Richeson, daughter Kawai, daughter Shandara, and son Michael.

three of us at once how remarkable it was that here we were, three people who grew up in totally different parts of the world, mortally afraid of each other…sitting in an outpost in space together, working together and getting along just great."

Shannon Lucid's return to gravity was also going great. She rested for a few days after getting home and then started an exercise program to regain her former strength. She had lost a little mass from her bones and muscles while on *Mir*, but did not suffer any major problems. She said: "There were a lot of muscles I didn't use in space. It took a little while to get used to using them again, but I haven't had any muscle pain, so my exercise program on *Mir* must have worked very well."

When she went back to her office at the space center, piles of mail greeted her. She had hundreds of requests for public appearances and interviews. She accepted some of them, but had to finally draw the line and get back to work. At home Lucid said that she was "...getting a lot of enjoyment out of simple things like cooking for my family, doing laundry, cleaning house, and talking to friends."

After Shannon Lucid's first shuttle mission her husband, Mike, said: "I'm just glad Shannon has the opportunity to do what she wants to do. There are so many people who go through life and don't get the chance. Her job has its rewards and disappointments, its ups and downs. The only difference might be that her ups are a little higher."

Lucid agrees and says that she has "...the best job in the world." When she was asked about her future in space, Shannon Lucid said: "I would really hope to see the day in the future when we would be able to make a flight to Mars. And I'd love to be on it."

IMPORTANT DATES

1943 Shannon Wells born in China on January 14.

1957 Russian satellite, *Sputnik I*, orbits Earth on October 4.

1960 Graduates from high school.

1963 Earns B.S. degree in chemistry from the University of Oklahoma.

1968 Daughter Kawai Dawn born on September 19.

1970 Daughter Shandara Michelle born on January 13; Lucid earns M.S. degree in biochemistry from the University of Oklahoma.

1973 Earns Ph.D. in biochemistry from the University of Oklahoma.

1975 Son Michael born on August 22.

1978 NASA accepts first women astronaut candidates.

1979 Becomes one of first six women astronauts.

1985 Flies aboard *Discovery* mission STS-51G.

1989 Flies aboard *Atlantis* mission STS-34.

1991 Flies aboard *Atlantis* mission STS-43.

1993 Flies aboard *Columbia* mission STS-58.

1996 Liftoff for six months aboard *Mir*, March 22; returns to Earth September 26.

FURTHER READING

Armbruster, Ann, and Elizabeth Taylor. *Astronaut Training*. New York: Franklin Watts, 1990.

Bredeson, Carmen. *Gus Grissom: A Space Biography*. Springfield, NJ: Enslow, 1997.

Markle, Sandra. *Pioneering Space.* New York: Atheneum, 1992.

Naden, Corinne J., and Rose Blue. *Christa McAuliffe: Teacher in Space*. Brookfield, CT: Millbrook, 1991.

Neal, Valerie, Cathleen Lewis, and Frank Winter. *Spaceflight: A Smithsonian Guide*. New York: Prentice-Hall Macmillan, 1995.

Ride, Sally. *To Space and Back*. New York: Lothrop, Lee & Shepard Books, 1986.

Vogt, Gregory. *Space Stations*. New York: Franklin Watts, 1990.

INDEX